From Daybreak to Good Night

Poems for children by Carl Sandburg

Art by Lynn Smith-Ary

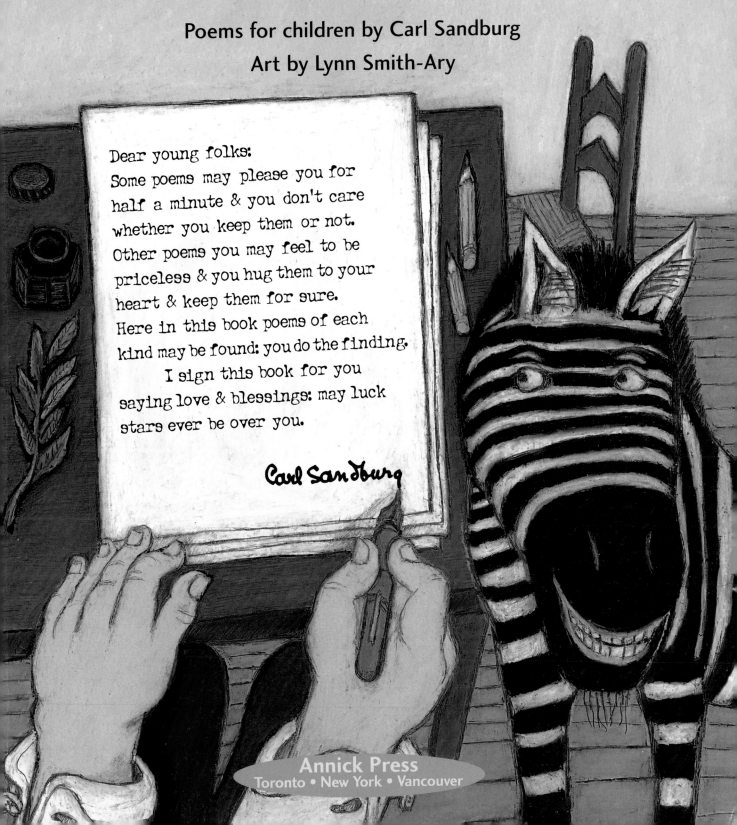

Dear young folks:
Some poems may please you for half a minute & you don't care whether you keep them or not. Other poems you may feel to be priceless & you hug them to your heart & keep them for sure. Here in this book poems of each kind may be found: you do the finding.
    I sign this book for you saying love & blessings: may luck stars ever be over you.

Carl Sandburg

Annick Press
Toronto • New York • Vancouver

Should children write poetry?
Yes, whenever they feel like it.

—Carl Sandburg

Carl Sandburg (1878–1967), the distinguished and much-loved American poet and writer, lived the last 22 years of his life with his family on a farm called Connemara in Flat Rock, North Carolina. Sandburg described his farm as "240 acres and a million acres of sky," and would often take walks along the winding paths or through the woods.

There were always lots of visitors at Connemara, many of them children, who were sometimes treated to a singalong led by the poet.

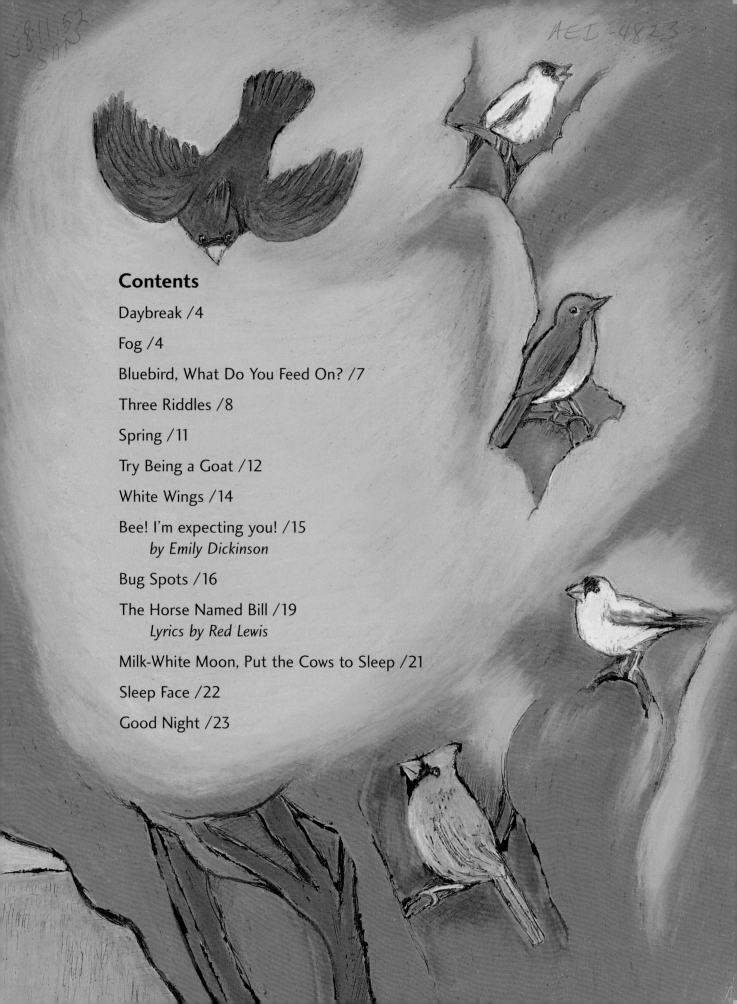

Contents

Daybreak

Daybreak comes first
    in thin splinters shimmering.
Neither is the day here
    nor is the night gone.
Night is getting ready to go
And Day whispers, "Soon now, soon."

Fog

The fog comes
on little cat feet.

It sits looking
over harbor and city
on silent haunches
and then moves on.

4

Bluebird, What Do You Feed On?

Bluebird, what do you feed on?
It is true you gobble up worms, you
    swallow bugs,
And your bill picks up corn, seed,
    berries.
This is only part of the answer.
Your feathers have captured a piece of
    smooth sky.
Your wings are burnished with
    lake-morning blue.
It is not a worm blue nor a bug
    blue nor the blue
Of corn or berry you shine with.
Bluebird, we come to you for facts,
    for valuable
Information, for secret reports.
Bluebird, tell us, what do you
    feed on?

Three Riddles

Riddle 1
If you ask your mother for one fried egg for breakfast and she gives you two fried eggs and you eat both of them, who is better in arithmetic, you or your mother?

Riddle 2

There was a zebra with 5 stripes on one side
and 6 stripes on the other. He got sick and lost
one stripe. How many had he left?

Riddle 3

There are 10 apples in a blue wheelbarrow.

      12 apples in a white   "

      4 apples in a red   "

      2 apples in a pink   "

How many apples are there in the blue wheelbarrow?

Spring

Spring is when the grass turns green and glad.
Spring is when the new grass comes up and says, "Hey, hey!
   Hey, hey!"
Be dizzy now and turn your head upside down and see how
   the world looks upside down.
Be dizzy now and turn a cartwheel, and see the good earth
   through a cartwheel.

Tell your feet the alphabet.
Tell your feet the multiplication table.
Tell your feet where to go, and watch 'em go and come back.

Can you dance a question mark?
Can you dance an exclamation point?
Can you dance a couple of commas?
And bring it to a finish with a period?

Try Being a Goat

Try being a goat: put on a face of calm contemplations.
Look people in the eye as though unaware they gaze at you.
    Read their innermost hidden secrets.
Then turn away toward other horizons chewing your cud.

12

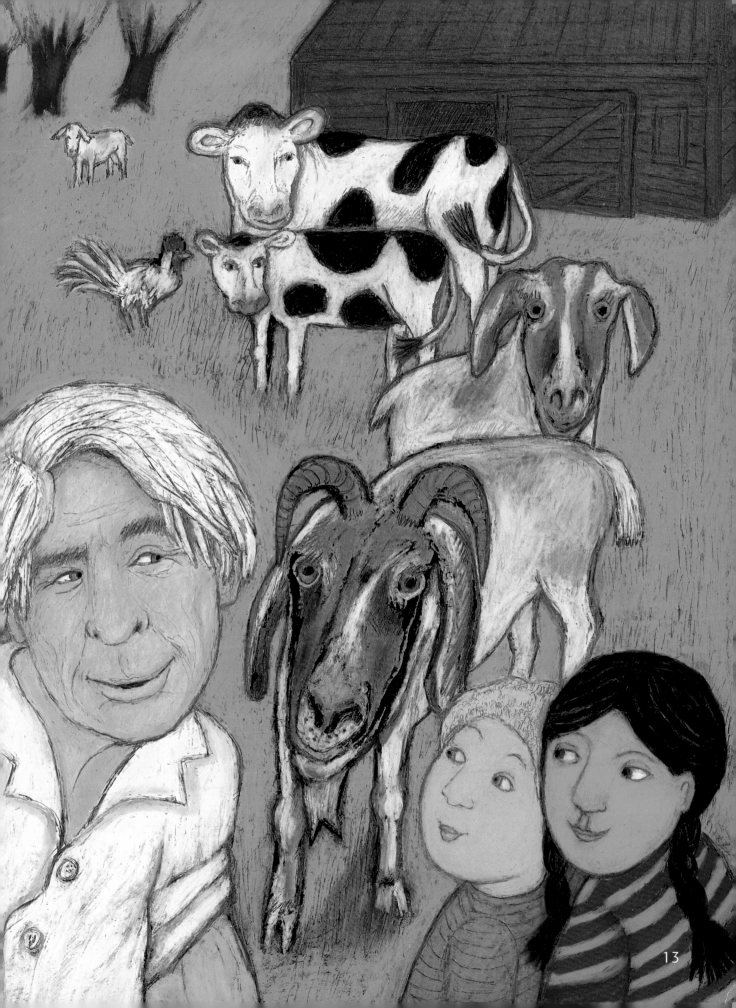

White Wings

Sitting against a big friendly tree
Reading a book I love,
I looked up suddenly
And saw fleeting and wheeling
Away in the blue spring sky
A flock of gray birds
Flashing white wings in the May sun.

14

Bee! I'm expecting you!
by Emily Dickinson

Bee! I'm expecting you!
Was saying Yesterday
To Somebody you know
That you were due –

The Frogs got Home last Week –
Are settled, and at work –
Birds, mostly back –
The Clover warm and thick –

You'll get my Letter by
The seventeenth; Reply
Or better, be with me –
Yours, Fly.

15

Bug Spots

This bug carries spots on his back.
Last summer he carried these spots.
Now it is spring and he is back here again
With a domino design over his wings.
All winter he has been in a bedroom,
In a hole, in a hammock, hung up, stuck away,
Stashed while the snow blew over
The wind and the dripping icicles,
The tunnels of frost.
Now he has errands again in a rotten stump.

The Horse Named Bill
Lyrics by Red Lewis

Oh, I had a horse and his name was Bill,
And when he ran he couldn't stand still.
He ran away—one day—
And also I ran with him.

Milk-White Moon, Put the Cows to Sleep

Milk-white moon, put the cows to sleep.
Since five o'clock in the morning,
Since they stood up out of the grass,
Where they slept on their knees and hocks,
They have eaten grass and given their milk
And eaten grass again and given milk,
And kept their heads and teeth at the earth's face.
  Now they are looking at you, milk-white moon.
  Carelessly as they look at the level landscapes,
  Carelessly as they look at a pail of new white milk,
  They are looking at you, wondering not at all, at all,
  If the moon is the skim face top of a pail of milk,
  Wondering not at all, carelessly looking.
  Put the cows to sleep, milk-white moon,
  Put the cows to sleep.

Sleep Face

You have a thousand wake faces and you can pick any wake face you want. But your sleep face is when you are you, and if you could see your sleep face you would say, "Of all my thousand faces, this one is me."

Good Night

Many ways to spell good night.

Fireworks at a pier on the Fourth of July
    spell it with red wheels and yellow spokes.
They fizz in the air, touch the water and quit.
Rockets make a trajectory of gold-and-blue
    and then go out.

Railroad trains at night spell with a smokestack mushrooming a white
    pillar.

Steamboats turn a curve in the Mississippi crying in a baritone that crosses
    lowland cottonfields to a razorback hill.

It is easy to spell good night.
                    Many ways to spell good night.

We acknowledge the support of the Canada Council for the Arts, the Ontario Arts Council, and the Government of Canada through the Book Publishing Industry Development Program (BPIDP) for our publishing activities.

Cataloging in Publication Data

Sandburg, Carl, 1878-1967
  From daybreak to good night : poems for children

ISBN 1-55037-681-0 (bound)   ISBN 1-55037-680-2 (pbk.)

1. Farm life – Juvenile poetry. 2. Children's poetry, American.
I. Smith-Ary, Lynn, 1942- . II. Title.

PS3537.A618F76 2001   j811'.52   C2001-930079-4

The art in this book was rendered in crayon on acetate, photocopied, and then further enhanced with additional crayons and colored pencils.
The text was typeset in Charlotte Sans.

Distributed in Canada by: Published in the U.S.A. by Annick Press (U.S.) Ltd.
Firefly Books Ltd.   Distributed in the U.S.A. by:
3680 Victoria Park Avenue   Firefly Books (U.S.) Inc.
Willowdale, ON   P.O. Box 1338
M2H 3K1   Ellicott Station
                               Buffalo, NY 14205

Printed and bound in Canada by
Friesens, Altona, Manitoba.

visit us at: www.annickpress.com

A Note from the Illustrator
Almost forty years ago, Carl Sandburg kindly answered a letter I had sent him as a teenager. His words of encouragement were inspiring, and in some way led to the idea for this book and to the selection of these poems. I still have his letter, stored in a very safe place.

About the zebras in the book: the truth is, there never really were any zebras at Connemara. But remember, Carl Sandburg was a poet and a dreamer who wrote about zebras from time to time, so he may have imagined a zebra roaming around the farm.

To my parents, Dr. & Mrs. Alexander B. Smith, to my husband, Zander Ary, and to Margaret McAlpine
—L.S-A.

"Daybreak", "Fog", "Bluebird, What Do You Feed On?", "White Wings", "Bug Spots", "Milk-White Moon, Put the Cows to Sleep", "Good Night", excerpts from "Arithmetic" ("Riddle 1"), and "Lines Written for Gene Kelly to Dance To" ("Spring"), originally published in *The Complete Poems of Carl Sandburg*.

Excerpt from "Dear Young Folks", originally published in *Wind Song*.

"Try Being a Goat" excerpted from "Breathing Tokens", and "White Wings" originally published in *Breathing Tokens*.

Excerpt from "The Horse Named Bill", Lyrics by Red Lewis, originally published in *The American Songbag*.

Excerpt from "Short Talk on Poetry" (p. 2), originally published in *Early Moon*.

"Bee! I'm expecting you!" reprinted by permission of the publishers and the Trustees of Amherst College from *The Poems of Emily Dickinson*, Thomas H. Johnson, ed., Cambridge, Mass.: The Belknap Press of Harvard University Press, © 1951, 1955, 1979 by the President and Fellows of Harvard College.

[Riddle 2] and [Riddle 3] from *Where Love Begins* by Helga Sandburg, © 1989 by Helga Sandburg. Used by permission of Donald I. Fine, an imprint of Penguin Putnam Inc.

Excerpts from *The Complete Poems of Carl Sandburg*, © 1970, 1969 by Lilian Steichen Sandburg, Trustee, reprinted by permission of Harcourt, Inc.

Excerpt from *Wind Song*, © 1960 by Carl Sandburg and renewed 1988 by Margaret Sandburg, Janet Sandburg, and Helga Sandburg Crile, reprinted by permission of Harcourt, Inc.

Excerpts from *Breathing Tokens*, © 1978 by Maurice C. Greenbaum and Frank M. Parker, Trustees of the Sandburg Family Trust and Harcourt, Inc., reprinted by permission of the publisher.

Excerpt from *The American Songbag*, © 1927 by Harcourt, Inc., and renewed 1955 by Carl Sandburg, reprinted by permission of the publisher.

Excerpt from *Early Moon*, © 1930 by Harcourt, Inc., and renewed 1958 by Carl Sandburg, reprinted by permission of the publisher.

Excerpt from "Sleep Face" reprinted with permission of The Trustees of the Carl Sandburg Family Trust.

Special thanks to Helga Sandburg Crile for all her support and suggestions throughout the production of this book.

Back cover photograph of Carl Sandburg:
A *Washington Post* photograph by Ellsworth Davis.
Back cover photograph of Lynn Smith-Ary:
Michael Pinsonneault